MARGRET & H. A. REY'S

Curious George
Visits the Dentist

written by Monica Perez

illustrated in the style of H. A. Rey *by* Mary O'Keefe Young

HOUGHTON MIFFLIN HARCOURT

Boston   New York

For Delma and Angel, with love and thanks
—M.P.

For our new Penny, with love
—M.O'K.Y.

www.hmhco.com
www.curiousgeorge.com

The text of this book was set in Adobe Garamond Pro.
The illustrations are watercolor with colored pencil.

ISBN 978-0-544-14611-2 hardcover
ISBN 978-0-544-14687-7 paperback
Printed in China
SCP 10 9 8 7 6 5 4 3 2 1
4500517343

George was a good little monkey and always very curious.

When he visited his neighbor Mrs. Ross, he was especially curious about her gleaming basket of fruit. That bright red apple on top looked too perfect to be true.

And it was! George bit into it and discovered that it was hard and sticky and not sweet.

"Oh, dear," said Mrs. Ross. "That's not a real apple, George. It's made of wax."

George's tooth began to hurt. "You should always ask before eating something, George," the man with the yellow hat reminded him.

By the time he went to bed that evening, George's tooth was less sore. But the next morning his tooth was wobbly!

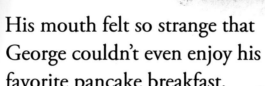

His mouth felt so strange that George couldn't even enjoy his favorite pancake breakfast.

"We should see the dentist, George," the man said. "She can make sure that tooth of yours is all right."

The man explained that the dentist was a doctor for
teeth, but George didn't want anyone to touch his tooth.
What if it hurt?

George walked along the path to the dentist's office with
his friend, his steps getting slower and slower until . . .
he ran off to pick a daisy.

"That's very pretty," said the man, chasing after George. "But we have an appointment and we shouldn't be late. You'll be a good little monkey, won't you?"

George nodded. He always wanted to be good.

The waiting room was a welcoming place.

There were lots of things to see and do. One by one, the young patients were called away by a woman in a white suit. George watched them go through a red door, each holding on to a grownup's hand.

One frightened boy was carried in by his mother. George was glad he wouldn't have to see the dentist by himself.

"George, you're next," the woman announced.
George was sad to put down his book, but he
was also a little curious about where the children
were going.

Was there a play area
on the other side?

The examining room was not filled with toys, but it was still interesting.

There was a sink and a long chair for lying down. There was a stool for the dentist and a light above the chair.

George was curious. Why were there two faucets in the room?

"Hello, George. I'm Dr. Wang. It's nice to meet you," she said. "Why don't you lie down and we'll take a look at your teeth?"

George saw a row of silver dental exam tools on the counter. They were long, shiny, and pointy. He hid behind the man.

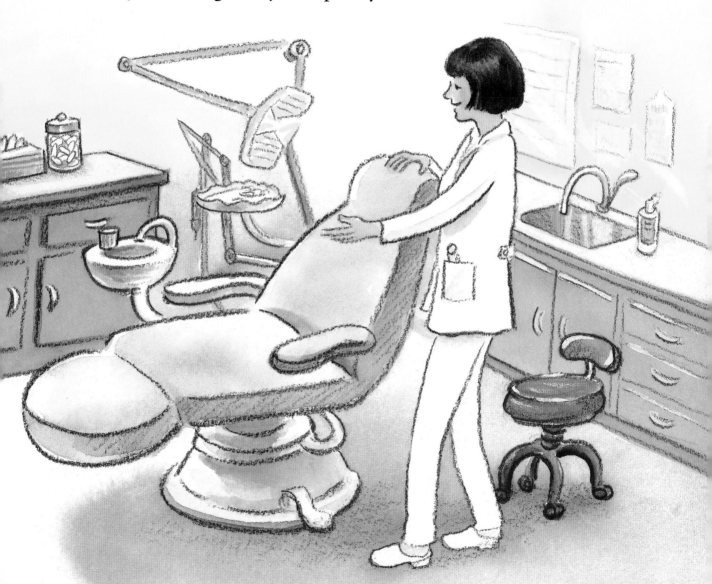

"George, would you like me to try out the chair first?" the man asked.

"Great idea!" said Dr. Wang.

The man lay down.
"Open your mouth wide." The dentist shined the big light down into the man's mouth. She took out a small white instrument to take a closer look at each tooth. "This is a mouth mirror."

George watched. It didn't look too scary.

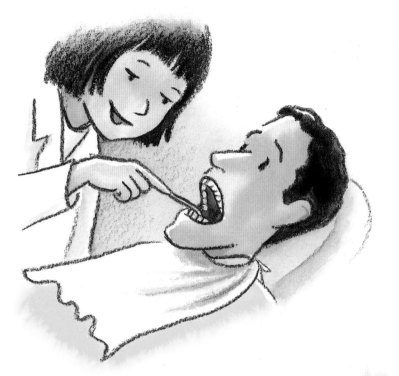

"Next I'll count the teeth,"
Dr. Wang told George.

She picked up one of those
sharp, pointy tools. "This
is an explorer. One, two,
three, four . . ."

Then the man exclaimed,
"Ow!"

"Uh-oh," the dentist said.

George ran away.

He left the exam room and scurried down the hall.
There were many doors. He didn't know which was the way out.

He tried one door and walked into another exam room.

"A monkey!" a little girl cried, and jumped off the exam
chair in excitement as George backed out of the room.

He continued down the hall, opening
doors and disturbing patients. In one
room the scared little boy from the
reception area was crying.

George had an idea.
He jumped onto a table and began
juggling packs of dental floss. The
little boy stopped crying and smiled.

Next George leaped over to the sink in the middle of the
room. He pushed a button and the nearby water jet spurted,
spraying water around the room.

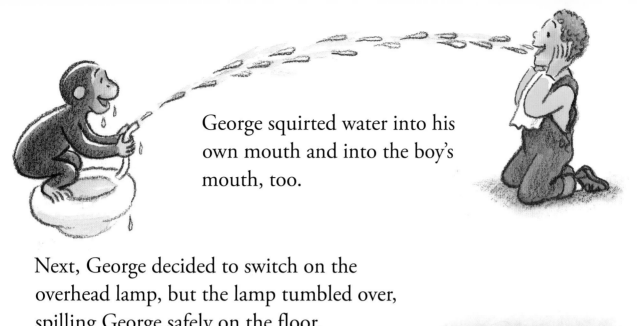

George squirted water into his own mouth and into the boy's mouth, too.

Next, George decided to switch on the overhead lamp, but the lamp tumbled over, spilling George safely on the floor.

The boy clapped.

But . . . uh-oh. Dr. Wang stood in the doorway.

"George, you naughty monkey!" Dr. Wang said. "What a mess you've made."

"This monkey was the only one who could get Tyler to stop crying," the boy's mother said.

"Hmm." Dr. Wang considered. She said, "It does look like we have some eager young patients. And if it weren't for you, George, I wouldn't have found the cavity in your friend's mouth."

"Turns out I need to have a filling," the man with the yellow hat said. "Come on, George, let's both get our teeth checked!"

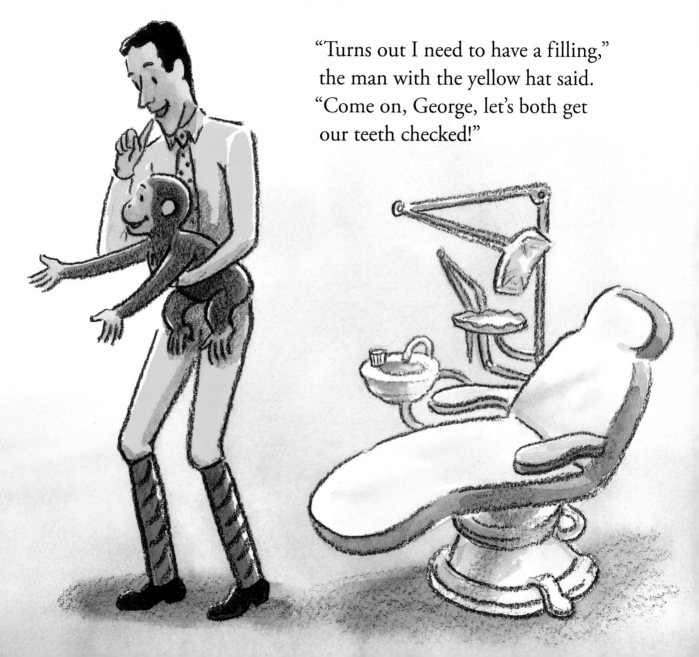

As soon as Dr. Wang looked into George's mouth, she laughed. "Why, George, all you have is a loose tooth!" A loose tooth sounded worrisome to George. "It's going to fall out soon. There's a new, permanent tooth right behind it. Looks like you've been doing a good job brushing your teeth."

George jumped on his chair. He did. He brushed every night and morning.

"Keep brushing and don't eat too many sweets," the dentist reminded him.
"You want your teeth to be in good shape for the tooth fairy."

George waved goodbye to his new friends. He went home with a new toothbrush, some dental floss, and instructions for his loose tooth—he should bite into as many hard apples as he could, as long as they were real, of course.

He decided he didn't mind going to the dentist at all. That night he ate a healthy dinner with an apple for dessert. His tooth fell out with his second bite.

He put his tooth under his pillow.

The next morning George found a special coin in his tooth's place.

When Mrs. Ross came to check on George that afternoon, George proudly showed her his coin from the tooth fairy. Mrs. Ross laughed and said, "Well, that was a quick way to lose a tooth. But I don't recommend it next time!"